D1761715

Make the World a Better Place!

My Sharing Time, Talent, and Treasure Activity Book

by Elizabeth Flikkema

Layout and Illustrations by Christian Olsen

This Book Belongs to:

_____

**LEARNING
TO GIVE**
AN ACTION OF THE HEART
A PROJECT FOR THE MIND

Learning to Give is an innovative educational initiative seeking to maintain and enhance civil society. This philanthropy education program is designed to be infused in Pre-K to 12th grade classrooms with seamless connections to core curricular standards.

Learning to Give:

- *EDUCATES* youth about philanthropy, the nonprofit and volunteer sector, and the importance of giving their time, talent and treasure for the common good (knowledge),
- *DEVELOPS* philanthropic behavior and experience (skills), and,
- *EMPOWERS* youth to take voluntary citizen action for the common good in their classrooms, their lives and their communities (behavior).

Published by Learning to Give Press: Muskegon, Michigan

For information, contact:
Learning to Give
630 Harvey Street
Muskegon, MI 49442
www.learningtogive.org

ISBN 0-9774155-0-3

Hello, I'm your ant—Ant Philomena —but you can call me Ant Phil. You know that ants are small, but we are strong. You are also very powerful. You have what it takes to make the world a better place. I'm here to teach you how.

Ant Phil belongs to an ant community that works together for the common good. She has a lot to teach about "Phil-Ant-thropy."

Follow her trail and scout out the activities. By the end of this book, you will be connected to your community in many ways, creatively sharing your time, talent, and treasure to make your world a better place. That's philanthropy!

Philanthropy: giving time, talent, and treasure, and taking action for the common good

Common Good

Do you know someone who . . .

seems to understand and care about how other people feel?

is good at sharing and taking turns?

spends time helping others?

is good at something and likes teaching others?

cares about everyone being treated fairly?

follows the rules?

cares about the environment?

Maybe one of these describes YOU! People who do these things care about the common good.

We all care about the common good. You probably don't even think about it. Write your thoughts about the people around you—your family, your neighbors, your friends and classmates. How do you act in ways that are good for them, and how do they act in ways that are good for you and everyone?

_____

_____

_____

_____

_____

Common good: acting in a way that is good for everybody (the community)

ABCs of Giving

Read about some ways kids can give for the common good.

A Ask a neighbor if you may help with a project.

B Bake something for a soup kitchen.

C Care for a sick animal.

D Donate a book to the library.

E Encourage a child who is learning a new skill.

F Form a "kids care" club with your friends.

G Give a helping hand.

H Help clean up trash in a common area.

I Illustrate a picture for someone.

J Join others who are already helping.

K Kindly ask if you may help someone.

L Listen to and respect people.

M Make something special for someone you like.

N Notice if someone needs help.

O Offer to help a neighbor.

P Participate in a fund raiser.

Q Quietly share when it isn't expected.

R Remember your manners without reminders.

S Say hello to people.

T Teach about caring by example.

U Understand how someone feels.

V Volunteer at a school function.

W Warmly welcome a guest or new student.

X Explain what philanthropy means to you.

Y Yell "yes" to sharing time, talent and treasure.

Z Zip up someone's coat.

What Is Philanthropy?

Philanthropist: a person who shares or gives time, talent, or treasure or takes action for the common good.

Read the examples. Write yes or no to tell if it describes an act of philanthropy.

- If yes, circle time, talent, or treasure. (You may circle more than one.) On the lines, write about who else in the example is acting philanthropically.
- If no, write about why the act is not an example of philanthropy.

Yesenia and her friends planted flowers around the community park. The community provided the flowers, but the friends did not get paid for their work. Are Yesenia and her friends philanthropists? _____ Are they sharing time, talent, or treasure? _____

_____

_____

Ms. Featherboa gave ten boxes of leftover fabric from her purse factory to a local quilting group. The quilting group makes quilts for homeless families. Is Mrs. Featherboa acting as a philanthropist?_____ Is she sharing time, talent, or treasure? _____

_____

_____

Pedro earns $15 for each lawn he mows in his neighborhood. Is Pedro acting as a philanthropist?_____ Is he sharing time, talent, or treasure? _____

_____

_____

Keisha sings and plays the piano twice a year at a local church. She does not receive money for her playing. Is Keisha acting as a philanthropist?_____ Is she sharing time, talent, or treasure? _____

_____

_____

Giving Your Own Time, Talent, and Treasure

In each shape, write some acts of philanthropy YOU can do. Sort the following ideas into the correct shapes, then add your own ideas:

- donate some used books

- recycle newspapers

- rake your neighbor's leaves

Time

_____

_____

_____

_____

_____

Treasure

_____

_____

_____

_____

_____

Talent

_____

_____

_____

_____

_____

ABCs of Giving II

Write your own ABCs of giving. Think of small and big things you can give or acts you can perform for others.

A _____

B _____

C _____

D _____

E _____

F _____

G _____

H _____

I _____

J _____

K _____

L _____

M _____

N _____

O _____

P _____

Q _____

R _____

S _____

T _____

U _____

V _____

W _____

X _____

Y _____

Z _____

Think of a compliment someone gave you. What did you like about it?

_____

We can compliment actions,

"You played soccer well today."

behavior,

"Shawn listened well to my story."

a completed work,

"Great picture of a penguin!"

or an attitude

"You seem happy today"

Look at the cartoon. Which compliment is more meaningful and kind? Why?

Write a real compliment that you could give to each person listed below (use a name if possible).

The texture makes your sculpture look so real.

I like your sculpture.

Someone in your family _____
_____

Someone in your neighborhood _____
_____

A classmate _____
_____

Someone who works at your school _____
_____

Someone younger than you _____
_____

Try It!   Give at least one compliment each day this week.

What Is a Friend?

Friends are part of your community.

In your own words, write what you think a friend is.

_____

_____

Name three things a friend might do for a friend.

_____

_____

Write about a time you shared with a friend.

_____

_____

What does it mean to trust a friend?

_____

_____

Describe how you feel when someone trusts you.

_____

_____

Draw yourself with a friend doing something for the common good.

What might someone who acts like a friend look like? Complete the picture and label the body parts with acts of friendship. For example, eyes for watching out for each other.

I'm Sorry

"It is easier to forgive an enemy than a friend."
–Madame Dorothèe Deluzy, French Actress (1747-1830)

"The weak can never forgive. Forgiveness is the attribute of the strong."
–Mahatma Gandhi, Indian Activist and Philosopher (1869-1948)

"To err is human; to forgive, divine."
Alexander Pope, Essayist, Critic, and Poet (1688-1744)

Saying "I'm sorry" and forgiving someone can be difficult. Read the quotes above and write your own thoughts about the following ideas:

Why is it difficult to say "I'm sorry"?

_____

_____

How do you feel when you make a mistake?

_____

_____

What does it mean to forgive a friend or family member? What does it look and sound like?

_____

_____

How do you feel after you say "I'm sorry"?

_____

_____

"No one has a right to consume happiness without producing it."
–Helen Keller, Advocate for the deaf and blind
(1880-1968)

Life, like a mirror, never gives back more than we put into it.
(Anonymous)

"Nobody needs to wait a single moment before starting to improve the world."
–Anne Frank, German-Jewish writer
(1929-1945)

"Happiest are the people who give most happiness to others."
–Denis Diderot, philosopher (1713-1784)

**"Ask not what your country can do for you ...
Ask what you can do for your country."**
–John F. Kennedy, 35th President of the United States
(1917-1963)

What Does it Mean?

Read the quotes on page 13 and choose your favorite one. Write about what it means to you.

"I think it means that promoting philanthropy propagates propriety."

What does the quote mean to you?

_____

_____

What does the quote tell you about your responsibility to be a philanthropist?

_____

_____

What can you give besides money?

_____

_____

Write your own short and catchy phrase that tells how you feel about giving. (This might make a nice poster for your bedroom or family refrigerator.)

_____

_____

_____

_____

My Money

How do you get money?

_____

What do you like to do when you have money?

_____

_____

There are three things you can do with your money:

Spend: using money for something you want or need.

Save: keeping the money for future wants or needs.

Donate: giving the money to someone for the common good.

Write one or more ideas to answer the following questions.

On what do you like to *spend* your money?

_____

_____

For what future purchase(s) would you like to *save* your money?

_____

_____

About what issue do you care enough to want to *donate* your money?

_____

_____

Making a Plan

There are three things you can do with your money: spend it right away, save it for later, or donate it.

Some people make a plan like this:

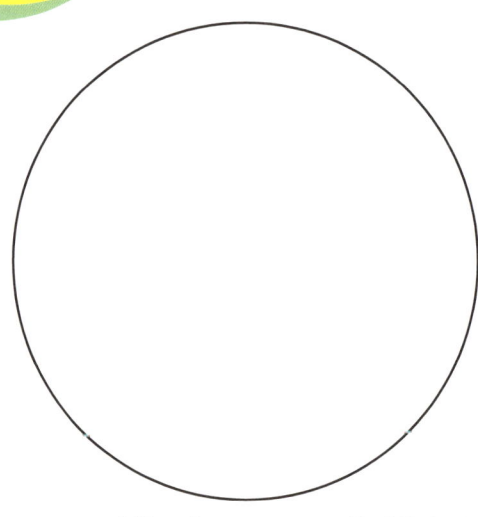

50% save for later

10% donate

40% spend,

Make a plan for how you would like to handle your money. Show how much of your money will go in each section.

Why do you think people choose to donate some of their money? (Think about how it is good for others and for the giver.)

_____

_____

_____

_____

"As the purse is emptied, the heart is filled."
–Victor Hugo, French writer
(1802-1885)

Art Project

Design a bank using recycled materials. Your bank should have three compartments: one for saving, one for current spending, and one for donating.

Choose the materials for the bank compartments. You will need three. Use cardboard tubes, shoe boxes, empty water bottles, milk cartons, chip tubes, empty checking account boxes, or deli containers.

Attach the containers and decide where the money can be dropped in each. You may need an adult to cut a hole.

Decorate the bank and label each container. Use ribbon, fabric scraps, drawer-liner adhesive paper, beads, buttons, glitter, and feathers.

You Can Bank on Me

Sing to the tune of *"Do you know the Muffin Man?"*

Did you know you can bank on me, bank on me, bank on me?
Oh, did you know you can bank on me?
It's in the bank.

Did you know you could bank on me, bank on me, bank on me?
Oh, did you know you could bank on me?
It's there for you to spend.

Did you know you could bank on me, bank on me, bank on me?
Oh, did you know you could bank on me?
I'll help you save.

Did you know you can bank on me, bank on me, bank on me?
Oh, did you know you can bank on me?
I'll help you donate.

Did you know you can bank on me, bank on me, bank on me?
Oh, did you know you can bank on me?
You can count on me.

Try It! Write your own song about saving, spending, and donating.

Ten Dollars

Imagine that you unexpectedly get $10. Write a poem (or song or rap) about different ways you could spend that $10. By the end of the poem, tell what you think you should do with the money. Your poem may include an explanation for how you got the $10.

_____

_____

_____

_____

_____

_____

_____

_____

_____

_____

_____

_____

_____

_____

 **Try It!** Try using a rhyme at the end of every other line. Alliteration (using words in a sentence that start with the same sound) and internal rhymes make it fun, too.

My Brilliant Idea

Imagine there is a contest for coming up with ideas to help people or animals in an important way. There is a prize of $1,000 for the best idea. Tell why you should get the money for your brilliant idea. Describe how the money will be spent and why it is important.

Your idea: _____

_____

_____

Who or what will be helped: _____

_____

_____

What will be the result: _____

_____

_____

How will the money be spent: _____

_____

_____

Why is it important: _____

_____

_____

_____

_____

Many philanthropists (people who make a difference for the common good) have done great things for their community and country. Honor their work by putting their faces on these coins. (They do not need to be famous to have done important work.) You are a philanthropist too! Make one coin with your face and information on it.

Include:
- a face
- the name beneath the face
- a word or phrase that describes the person or his/her work
- a date

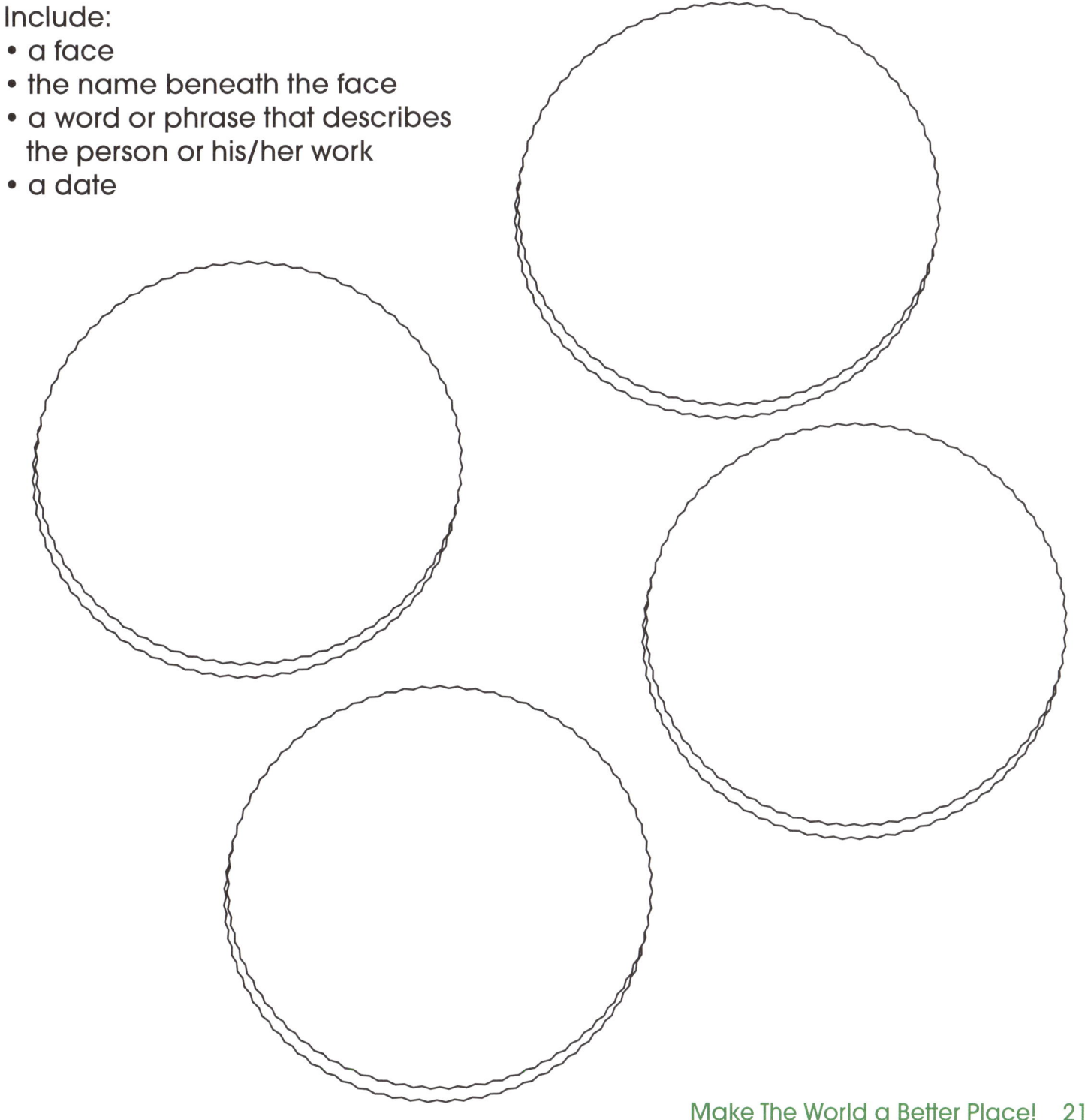

Write a Biography

Write about someone YOU KNOW who is a philanthropist. Include details to explain what the person did/does and why it is important.

Who: _____

_____

Describe the person: _____

_____

Act(s) of Philanthropy: _____

_____

Where: _____

_____

When: _____

_____

Why: _____

_____

This act of philanthropy is important to me because _____

_____

_____

_____

_____

Write your name on the trunk of the tree. Write the names of people who are close to you on the large branches. On the small branches, add other people who are part of your world. (Include people whose names you don't know. Such as the school crossing guard and the ice-cream store clerk.)

Think About It!

You are part of a community of people.
Do they all know each other?

Community Web

You are linked to your environment in a variety of ways. You influence nature and nature affects you. Draw a web of connections on this page.

Draw your home in the center of the page. Around your home, draw or write all of the places you go (park, friends' houses, school, etc.). Around each place, draw or write what you see, feel, smell, or meet on your way. Include animals, environments, pollution, other people, etc. Then draw lines connecting things that interact.

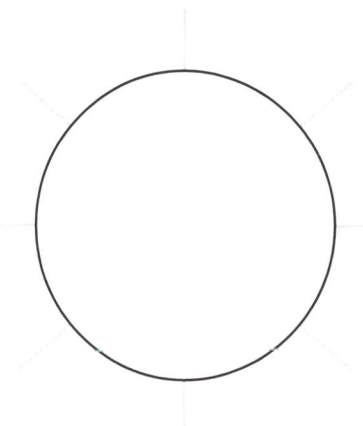

What does it mean to be connected to nature? What can you do for nature that benefits the common good?

What do you know about the community where you live? Draw a simple map of the center (or downtown) of your community. Include some of your favorite places. Label the streets and other interesting places on your map.

A community is a group of people living in the same area or a group having common interests

Community Philanthropists

Anthill at
Sunrise

Picantso
1904

Have you ever wondered who pays for the zoo or how museums afford expensive art and programs? The money comes from philanthropy in your own community.

How does the whole community benefit when someone donates money for a library, a park, a musical program, or a museum?

_____

_____

Why do people give money to community projects?

_____

_____

Is it the responsibility of each person or just rich people to give to their community? Why?

_____

_____

If you give $4 toward a new library, are you a philanthropist?

_____

A new playground in the park may have been purchased with money from a bake sale (treasure), built by volunteer parents (talent), and maintained by the Girl Scouts (time). Think about something your community needs or wants (a skate park, a new playground, a soccer field). What could YOU do to make it happen?

Visit the central area (or downtown) of your community. Look at buildings, parks, benches, statues, and homes. Think about who is paying for them.

- **Business:** places that are run for a profit of the owner
- **Government:** community projects or facility paid for by taxes
- **Philanthropy:** individuals, volunteers, and private foundations support these for the common good
- **Family:** personal money used to support single families, not the community

List the places you see on your walk under the sector that pays for it.

Business	Government	Philanthropy	Family
Shoe Store	Police Station	Food Pantry	My House

Community Needs and Wants

I need my beauty sleep.

What needs and wants are met in your community? Get the names of places from your chart on page 25. Write them in the appropriate circles.

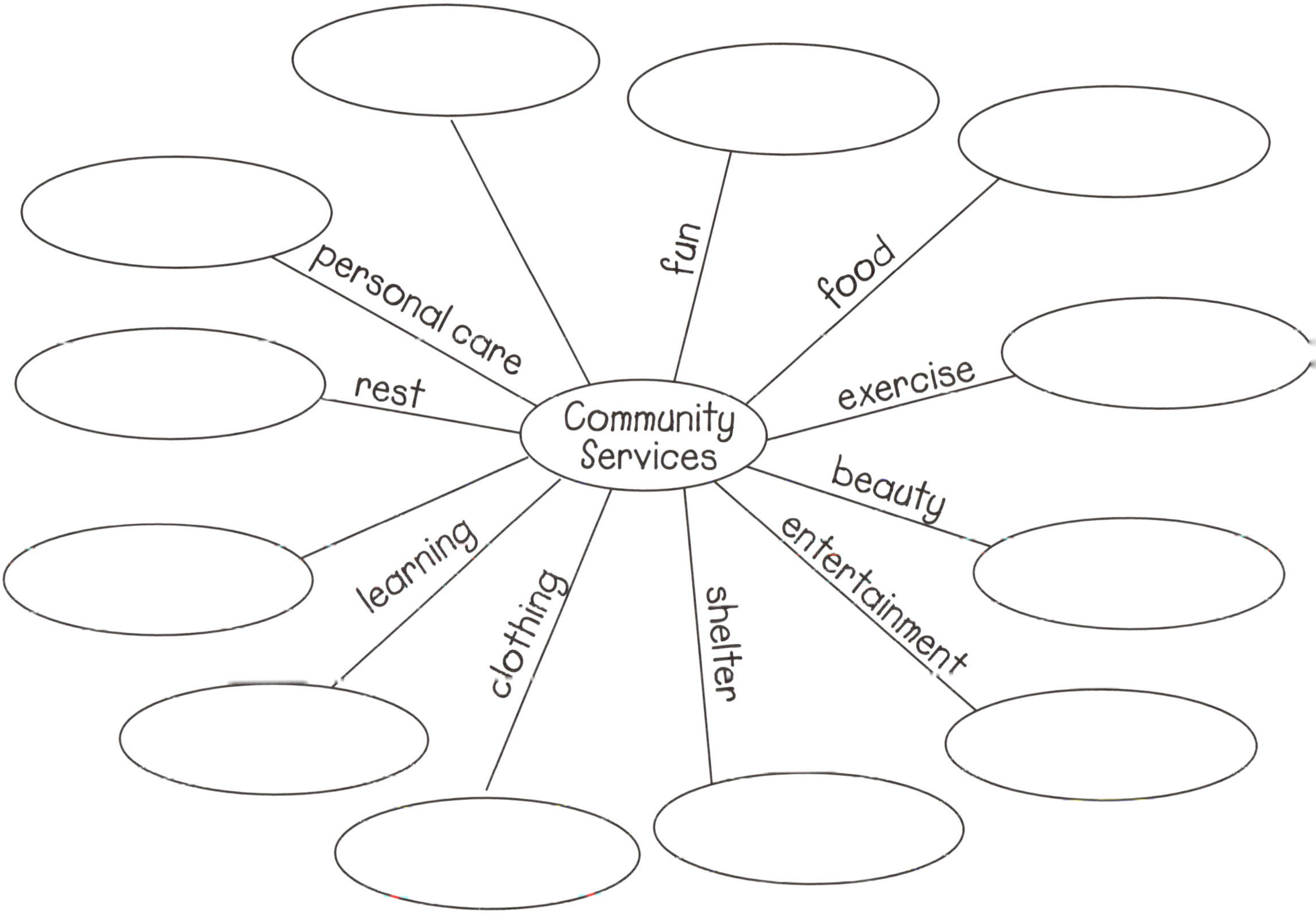

personal care

fun

food

rest

exercise

Community Services

beauty

learning

entertainment

clothing

shelter

Some buildings and statues have names engraved on them. Who are these people? Why are they important to your community? Make a list of the names you see on your community field trip. Add to the list some names of people you hear about who have supported the arts and other needs in the community.

Find out more about these people through interviewing and Internet research. Write about your findings.

Notes

_____

_____

_____

_____

_____

_____

_____

_____

Public Art

Draw a picture of a statue or piece of art that is part of your community.

Who paid for this piece of art and why?

_____

_____

How do people feel about this art? Decide how you will answer this question. You can ask your family. You can stand by the art and ask people how they feel. You can research the written opinions when the art was first displayed. How did you conduct your research?

_____

_____

Results of research:

_____

_____

_____

_____

_____

_____

_____

A community is formed any time a group of people gather for a common purpose. An example of a community may be a sports team, a scout troop, or a classroom. Belonging to a community can make you feel connected to others. Write about some communities to which you belong. Write how you benefit from the community and what you do for the community.

Community: _____
What I get from this community: _____
What I contribute to this community: _____

_____
_____
_____

Community: _____
What I get from this community: _____
What I contribute to this community: _____

_____
_____
_____

Community: _____
What I get from this community: _____
What I contribute to this community: _____

_____
_____
_____

Community: _____
What I get from this community: _____
What I contribute to this community: _____

_____
_____
_____

What Makes it Better?

Choose one community to which you belong and write it at the top. List the many things that make that community a good thing. At the bottom, list some things that would make the community even better. Highlight the ideas that YOU could do for the group.

_____
Name of Community

_____

_____

_____
Good Things About It

_____

_____

_____

_____

_____
Making It Better

Working together for the common good means getting along and compromising. How are you at problem solving? Circle how you would respond to each situation. Be honest.

Beth tells the Girl Scout troop her great idea for selling lemonade to raise money for a playground at a local school. You think that selling lemonade won't make enough money for such a big project, so you . . .

a. Tell her that it won't work.

b. Don't say anything about what you think.

c. Tell her you think a lemonade stand sounds fun, but think the group could choose something that makes more money.

Your soccer team is playing a game and you have played offense for two quarters. Your coach just told you to play offense for the third quarter, but you would like a new position, so you . . .

a. Storm off the field and tell the coach you won't play unless you get to be goalie.

b. Quietly go to your position, but sulk about it.

c. Explain your feelings and ask the coach politely if you may play a different position this quarter.

Your sister wants to play UNO again for the fourth night this week. You would like to play a different game, so you . . .

a. Throw the cards on the floor and say "I hate this game."

b. Play the game quietly and don't say anything.

c. Tell your sister you think it is your turn to choose the family game.

At recess, you are playing four square with a group of friends. You bounced the ball into Jack's square, but he didn't get it before it bounced again. He says that it wasn't a fair hit and wants you to do it again, so you . . .

a. Yell at him and tell him he is out.

b. Take the ball back and do the play again.

c. Tell Jack that you disagree and ask the other players to tell what they think. Then you go along with what most the people agree.

Results:

Mostly As: You tend to get angry and not listen to other people's ideas. Try to give as well as take when you disagree with someone.

Mostly Bs: You tend to hide your opinions and feelings from others. If you tell others your side, they can consider your point of view in the decision.

Mostly Cs: You are good at compromise. Listening to others and telling your point of view helps a group come up with a win-win solution.

I Can Solve a Problem

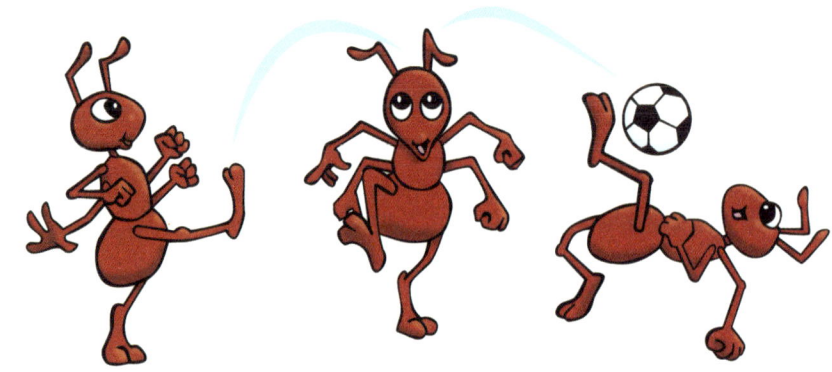

Write about a time when you helped solve a problem.

_____

_____

_____

_____

What did you do that made the situation better for everyone?

_____

_____

_____

_____

Write about a time when you left a problem unsolved.

_____

_____

_____

_____

What do you wish you had done differently?

_____

_____

_____

_____

There are many ways to be smart. Circle the words below that describe how you are smart. Star the one that seems the most like you.

Are you a person who . . .

 **Math Smart** solves logic problems and plays with numbers easily?

 **Music Smart** hears patterns in music and thinks about music?

 **Body Smart** likes to act or participate in sports or dance?

 **Nature Smart** is sensitive to the natural world?

 **Self Smart** knows yourself (what you can do and who you are)?

 **People Smart** understands other people?

 **Art Smart** pictures things in your head or can see how things fit together?

 **Word Smart** can use words well to express yourself?

"It is not enough to have a good mind. The main thing is to use it well."
–René Descartes, philosopher
(1596-1650)

What are My Interests?

Finish the sentences of the ideas that sound like you. Leave the other ones blank.

I like to play quietly with puzzles, dolls, or cars. I can spend lots of time by myself doing

_____
_____
_____

I'm very active. I like sports and staying busy. My favorite sport is

_____

I like doing things with my hands, like crafts and drawing. My favorite activity is

_____
_____

I want know to everything there is to know about

_____
_____

I collect things. My favorite things to collect are

_____
_____

I love to travel to new places and explore. My favorite place is

_____
_____

I like to play board games with my family and friends. My favorite game is

_____
_____

I like to read. My favorite time of day to read is

_____

My favorite books are

_____
_____

I'll do anything outside—gardening, looking in the pond, walking in the woods. You can usually convince me to go

_____
_____

I like to go places around town—like shopping and out for hot chocolate. My favorite place is

_____
_____

My Time, Talent, and Treasure

Reflect on your own time, talent, and treasure.

If I had an hour to spend on doing what I want to do for myself, I would like to...

_____
_____
_____

If I had an hour to spend doing things for the good of my community, I would like to use that time...

_____
_____
_____

I am really good at...

_____
_____
_____

One way that I can use my talent to help others is by...

_____
_____
_____

If I won $50, I would...

_____
_____
_____

If I won $50 and was trying to be a good steward/philanthropist, I would...

_____
_____
_____

What Can I Give?

Match your talents and interests (pages 35 and 36) with an issue. What issues are important to you? Animals? Nature? Hunger? Homelessness? Pollution? How can you make the world a better place?
Think about the following actions: entertain, teach, clean up, speak up, protect, support, and share.

Which of your talents could be used to address a natural issue such as pollution, endangered animals, or recycling?

_____

_____

_____

_____

Which of your talents could be used to help your neighbors?

_____

_____

_____

_____

Which of your talents could be used to help young children?

_____

_____

_____

_____

Which of your talents could be used to make your school, neighborhood, or community a better place?

_____

_____

_____

_____

Try it!

Choose just one of these ideas, make a plan, and DO IT!

My Family

Your family is important to you. It is the first place you learn to give for the common good.

What is one thing you like about your family?

_____

_____

_____

_____

Does your family ever disagree? Give some examples.

_____

_____

_____

_____

What does your family enjoy doing together?

_____

_____

_____

_____

How does your family solve small (and big) problems?

_____

_____

_____

_____

How does sharing help your family?

_____

_____

_____

_____

List some acts you can do to help make your home a better place.

_____

_____

_____

_____

Family Caring Container

Talk with your family about doing nice things for each other and the people in your neighborhood, school, or at work. Make a list of these things you can all do. Write each item from the list on a separate card. Fold the cards and put them in a large jar. Once a week, draw one card from the jar. Talk about how each of you can make it the focus for the week. After several days, talk about each person's experience.

Say please and thank you.

Offer to help someone who is upset.

Share a book with someone.

Respect each other's space.

Smile at others around you.

Compliment others around you.

Play with someone new.

Pick up any trash that you see on the floor.

Be willing to share.

Let someone know that you care about him or her.

Tell someone that you are his or her friend.

Bring a treat to school/work.

Write a letter to a friend.

Make a book for the class library.

Laugh with someone.

Say something nice to the principal.

Write a note to a school helper.

Work out a difference with someone.

My Community

Your school and community are important to you. What does the common good have to do with you?

What is one thing you like about your school or community?

_____
_____
_____
_____

What is one thing you would like to be better?

_____
_____
_____
_____

Whose responsibility is it to make it better? Why?

_____
_____
_____
_____

How does sharing help the school or community be better?

_____
_____
_____
_____

List some acts you can do to make your school or community a better place.

_____
_____
_____

Why is acting for the common good of the school or community your responsibility and not something extra?

_____
_____
_____
_____

Pass It On

There are no wrong answers here. Think creatively about passing kind acts on to others.

You are standing in line at the ice-cream store. The mom in front of you accidentally gets charged for your cone. You try to give her your money and she says, "I don't want your money, just pass it on." She wants you to pass on the kindness to someone else. What could you do? _____

_____

Your dad told you that you had to rake the leaves before the weekend was over. On Saturday morning you go outside and see that someone already did it. You're pretty sure your neighbor raked your leaves along with her own. What could you do? _____

_____

Last week, your friend helped you fix your bike. Today you go to his house to ask him to go bike riding with you, but he is babysitting his little sister. What could you do? _____

_____

Your grandma is in the hospital for a long time. Your mom and dad are busy helping her. Lots of neighbors bring over meals for the family. You really appreciate their help, but they don't want anything in return. What can you do?

_____

_____

You watch a nature show on television about some endangered wolves. You feel sad about the loss of their homes. You read about groups of people who are working to help the wolves and other endangered animals. What can you do?

_____

_____

_____

"The point is not to pay back kindness but to pass it on."
Julia Alvarez, contemporary author

Each month, you and your family can choose a focus and do something special.

Philanthropy Calendar

January

March of Dimes Birth Defects Prevention Month. Raise awareness about children's health issues by making posters or raising money in the neighborhood.

February

Black History Month. Read about African-American contributions to our history and society. Discuss the philanthropic contributions of African-Americans—such as those involved in the underground railroad—and the role of the NAACP as a nonprofit organization.

March

National Women's History Month. Celebrate the roles of women throughout history. Read about women in your community who are involved in philanthropy.

April

Keep America Beautiful Month. Take personal responsibility about proper waste disposal, environmental improvement and litter prevention. Earth Day is April 22.

May

Asian-Pacific American Month. Recognize the contributions and celebrate the culture of Asian-Pacific Americans.

June

National Family Month. Celebrate the family as "first communities." Make posters promoting strong families for healthy kids. Study a family that you greatly admire or interview relatives regarding their involvement in philanthropy, either as recipients or as donors.

July

National Recreation and Parks Month. Use park facilities in your area. Volunteer to work a day in the park!

August

National Back-to-School Month. Read about organizations that help provide school supplies and clothes for needy children.

September

National Grandparents Day. Celebrate with gift giving and recognition of grandparents and other elderly people in your community.

October

National Animal Safety and Protection Month. Learn about caring for animals through a trip the humane society or local zoo, viewing movies about animals, or doing something special for a family pet.

November

Election Day. Visit a polling place. Hold a "get out the vote" rally. Discuss the importance of freedom of speech and assembly. Celebrate Hispanic Heritage Month and National American Indian month.

December

The holidays of Ramadan, Hannukkah, Christmas and Kwanza offer opportunities to discuss peace, justice and caring. Organize a giving project by making or collecting gifts for the "unknown other" through a local shelter or service group.

Let's Decide!

Use the decision-making model to help you choose a giving project using money you have saved.

	Criteria: What factors are important to you? (examples: cost; number of people it helps; time; Is it fun?)			
Choices (List down the column.)				

Decision-Making Model Steps

1. Select choices (Write project ideas down the first column.)
2. Determine criteria (Write four factors that could make the projects easy or difficult.)
3. Rate/Evaluate (Develop a scale and assign numbers to each box.)
4. Make a decision.

A **haiku** poem is a "picture poem" that doesn't rhyme. It is often about nature. A haiku has three lines with 17 syllables, or beats.

Line 1 has 5 beats

Line 2 has 7 beats

Line 3 has 5 beats

Sample:

Give time and talent
To animals of the earth.
Share your joy of life.

Beautiful stream
Home to animals and plants
Keep it clean and pure.

Write your own haiku about giving, especially related to the environment.

_____

_____

_____

Write a Cinquain

A *cinquain* is a five-line poem that does not rhyme and is set up like this:

Line 1 is a single word (usually a noun)

Line 2 has two words (usually 2 adjectives)

Line 3 has three words (usually verbs ending in –ing)

Line 4 has a descriptive 4-word phrase

Line 5 is a single word (usually a synonym for the first word or repeats it)

Sample:

Global Community

Giving

Heart, mind

Sharing, caring, empowering

Helps our global community

Love

Write your own cinquain about giving.
(Provide lines in the diamond shape of the cinquain poem.)

_____

_____

_____

_____

_____

Write your observations related to making the world a better place.

Person that I helped and what I did

Person who helped me

Do it! Make a philanthropy journal. Write and draw your thoughts as you grow as a philanthropist.

Contract of Commitment

I _____ do commit my time, talent, and
   (name)

treasure to the following philanthropic project:

_____

_____

_____

_____

My plan includes the following steps:

_____

_____

_____

_____

_____
signed

_____
date